David G. Henkin
and
James R. Barnes

WHO AM I? INDIVIDUAL INNOVATION

A Tale of Transitions, Conversations, and the Power of Possibilities

Copyright © 2014 by David G. Henkin and James R. Barnes

JB Innovation Press
112 Banbury Way, Wayne, PA 19087

jbinnovation.com

ISBN: 978-0-9789314-2-1

All rights reserved. No part of this publication may be reproduced, stored in a retrieval system or transmitted, in any form, or by any means, electronic, mechanical, recorded, photocopied, or otherwise, without the prior written permission of both the copyright owner and the above publisher of this book, except by a reviewer who may quote brief passages in a review.

The scanning, uploading, and distribution of this book via the Internet or via any other means without the permission of the publisher is illegal and punishable by law. Please purchase only authorized electronic editions and do not participate in or encourage electronic piracy of copyrightable materials. Your support of the author's rights is appreciated.

Printed in the United States of America

For Kerra and Brad
—D.G. Henkin

For Buff, Mike, Julie, Christie, Katie,
Andy, Henry, and Hemsley
—J.R. Barnes

Introduction. Missing Piece

We go through many transitions in life. People, organizations, businesses, and even society itself experiences transitions. Each transition can be perceived on a range of levels through different filters and experienced in different ways. Our ability to advance and achieve through transitions is vital to our growth and well-being.

In 1976, Shel Silverstein released a children's picture book titled *The Missing Piece*, followed by *The Missing Piece Meets the Big O* in 1981. The stories feature a circular creature that is missing a wedge-shaped piece of itself—essentially a circle with a pie piece missing. It doesn't like this "missing piece" and sets out in search of a means to complete itself.

The missing piece and its metaphor became a popular sensation. The notion that we as individuals may have a 'piece' missing may occur to us at any number of moments in our lives. While some may seldom or never feel an urge toward fulfillment, others live with a near constant yearning for it. The world can often appear as a palate of possibilities, and we pursue potential paths toward an elusive impression of fulfillment.

When do these moments occur? How do possibilities present themselves to us? Do they come knocking like opportunity? Are they hidden in the deeper breakdowns we experience? Are they right before us in the typical passage of life? In the transitions

we experience, surely many doors and windows open for our choosing—whether we actively open them or not.

However, as we have learned after recent decades of greater materialism and driving toward consumption, more is sometimes, but not always, better. What is the role of creativity and innovation in our individual path? As we will see, the idea of a missing piece is fit for a children's picture book, a CEO's leadership development program, a high school coaches' handbook, and any of the numerous domains where individual fulfillment and the ability to accelerate and achieve through transitions exists by harnessing possibilities and conversations.

We invite you to rouse your missing piece should one reside with or within you. That space can readily expand and contract, learn and grow, adapt and evolve. We have had the good fortune to be able to share the fable that follows. It is a peek into worlds with and without possibilities, missing conversations, real lives, and choices and consequences. We hope, dear reader, that you will enjoy these words as much as we have enjoyed writing them and that you will tether, tame, and leave free as serves your purpose.

PART ONE

1. Sleeping

"What day is it?"
"It's today," squeaked Piglet.
"My favorite day," said Pooh.
—A.A. Milne

I lie alone. So thinks Tanner Morgan as he defends against the coming day. His clock will alarm in moments, the sunlight already skewing his room into alternating patches of light beams and darkness. *I lie alone.*

At seventeen, Tanner no longer enjoyed slumber as he once did. Mornings used to be about waking up and departing from the welcoming cocoon of his bed into the outward day. Nowadays they were more about getting to school and steering around his family.

With his brother Steve in college, at least the upstairs bathroom was safely Tanner's to use. Though when Steve returned for a visit, Tanner usually found his toiletries had been thrown onto his bed. Tanner's mom, Amy, stopped offering to make anything for breakfast for her boys since she started back to work.

Noah James Johnson was Tanner's best friend since junior high—when they both found that many friends from elementary school didn't seem the same after the changeover to middle school. Noah James and Tanner met on the second day of junior high and happened to be in the same mental space in the new school experience: The added independence of having a locker, getting to classes without lining up, and so many older kids who looked like teenagers.

They also shared a bus route and began sitting together on the bus. This was a habit each had grown accustomed to, maybe even fond of, and anticipated.

Now they were juniors in high school, and the general routine seemed more important in some ways. As Tanner made his reluctant route through the morning, he added to his mental list the things to tell Noah James on the bus.

Tanner had been thinking about questions. Ms. Goodwin, his school's guidance counselor, had been talking with him about questions and how the root of "questions" is "quest." Are those seeking answers, or asking questions, on a quest? On a search? "Quest" reminded Tanner of adventure movies, epic novels, and the idea of some passionate thirsting for something beyond one's reach.

As far as Tanner was concerned, school had long been more about answers than questions ... and knowing the answers. He did not raise his hand very often but would regularly recite the answer to a question in his head. He sometimes would add a follow-up question or a question on a totally unrelated topic. As few answers as he offered, he asked even fewer questions.

But now, he felt like a quest was somehow forming around him. Questions formed in his mind. High school waited moments away as the bus pickup time approached. Uncertainty seemed to follow Tanner: questions about his outlook, not just his day ahead but life beyond high school, maybe even beyond college, maybe even beyond his family and his town and his friends. Something was waiting for him somewhere, he felt, but like early morning shadows and light to tired eyes, he could not see it clearly or make it tangible.

As he dashed to the bus, equally frustrated and annoyed, Tanner thought quickly about his first words to Noah James. Something was brewing somewhere and it seemed like a quest and a question were forming on the subject of his future.

> Well, your symptoms are consistant with a heavy case of Angst. Luckily this is the treatable kind, a sub-malaise known as Teenage Angst. Treatment includes ten years of experience and a loss of purity and ideals.

2. Wide Awake

Only the curious will learn and only the resolute overcome the obstacles to learning. The quest quotient has always excited me more than the intelligence quotient.
—Eugene S. Wilson

According to the system of left-brain or right-brain dominance, each side of the brain controls different types of thinking. Individuals are said to favor one type of thinking over the other. For example, a person who is more "left-brained" is often said to be more logical, analytical, and objective, while a person who is more "right-brained" is said to be more intuitive, thoughtful, and creative.

Tanner was not sure if he was more right or left brained, but the question lingered with him as he closed his locker and headed to class. Melanie Goodwin, the high school guidance counselor, had mentioned the left-brain / right-brain notion to Tanner while talking about life after high school and what to consider in picking a college, job, and even career.

Melanie was from the west coast, had an easy-going style, and was always ready with a comment, question, or example that seemed to both capture Tanner's vague feelings and specific worries. Her comments would often stick with him as thoughts in his mind on and off for days and sometimes even prompt discussions with Noah James.

Melanie recently motivated Tanner to the Internet to look up Audrey Hepburn when Melanie said, "Nothing is impossible. The word itself says 'I'm possible.' Go ask Audrey Hepburn."

With a weight heavier than usual appearing to be slumping Tanner's shoulders, Melanie asked Tanner to consider what was possible for him.

"Was Audrey Hepburn more left or right brained?" asked Tanner.

"Go find out, and see what possibilities were for Audrey while you're at it."

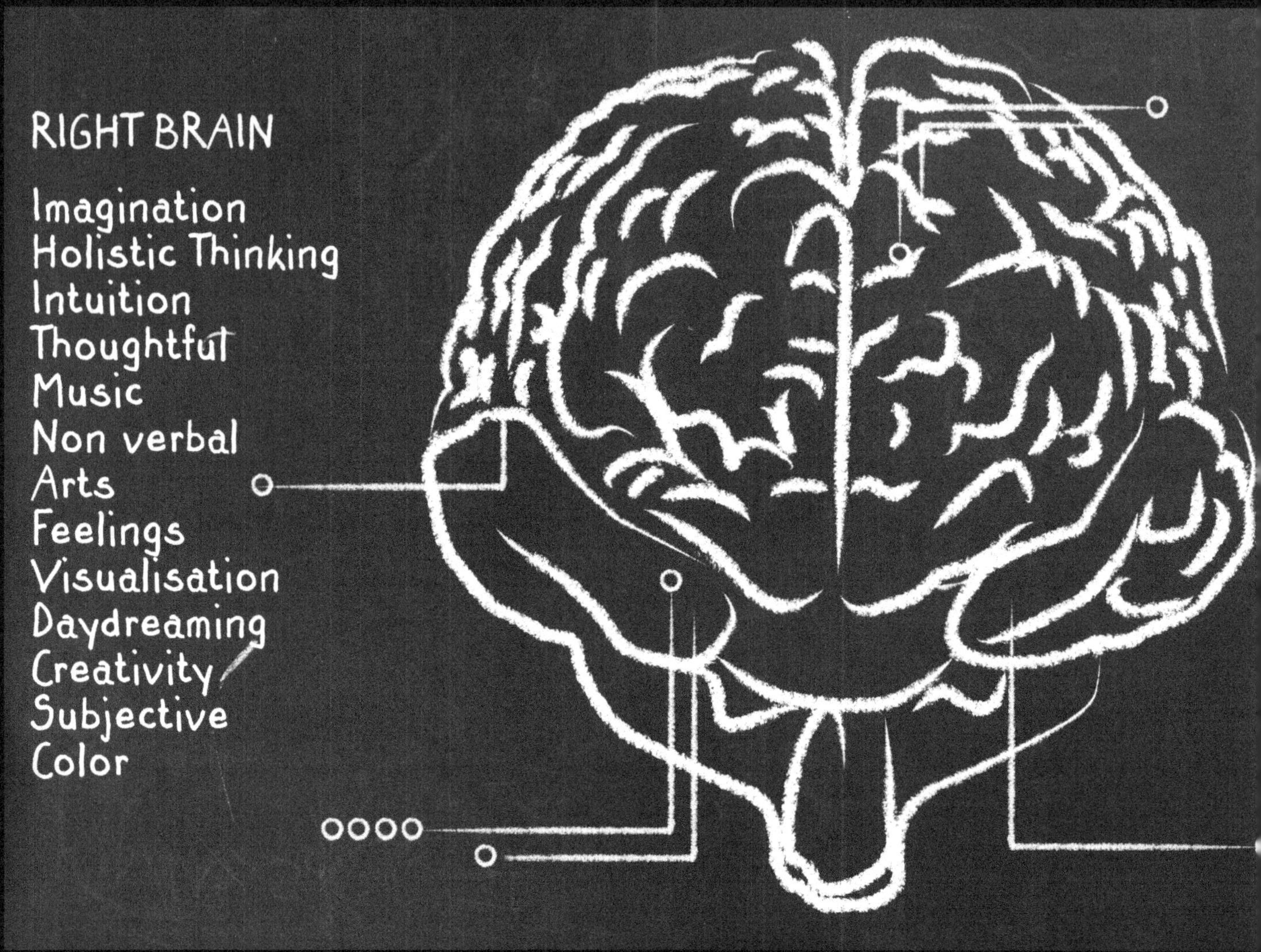

RIGHT BRAIN

Imagination
Holistic Thinking
Intuition
Thoughtful
Music
Non verbal
Arts
Feelings
Visualisation
Daydreaming
Creativity
Subjective
Color

Tanner learned from Melanie that there are three Types of conversation:

1. Conversations for **Understanding**

2. Conversations for **Possibilities**

3. Conversations for **Action**

Melanie would ask Tanner what type of conversation he wanted to have with her. Tanner was beginning to perceive how most conversations with his family, friends, and even strangers could be viewed as one type or another. This knowledge was both helping yet also making many conversations more problematic.

Among the many items on the wall of Ms. Goodwin's office, poet Shane Koyczan pointed his finger at what it's like to be young and different.

Tanner wasn't sure if he should be stirring or suppressing his brain's left or right side, his conversations, his expanding perspectives.

Whatever was happening to him—or going to happen—he was completely certain of this: change was coming, and the only path for him was forward.

LEFT BRAIN

Analysis
Linear
Logic
Mathematics
Language
Think in words
Words of songs
Computation
Facts
Sequencing
Objective
Reasoning
Numbers

I hid my heart under the bed because my mother said if you're not careful someday someone's gonna break it. Take it from me, under the bed is not a good hiding spot. I know because I've been shot down so many times I get altitude sickness just from standing up for myself. But that's what we were told, stand up for yourself. That's hard to do if you don't know who you are. We are expected to define ourselves at such an early age, and if we didn't do it, others did it for us. Geek. Fatty. Slut. Fag.

And at the same time we were being told what we were, we were being asked, "What do you want to be when you grow up?" I always thought that was an unfair question. It presupposes that we can't be what we already are. We were kids. ... They asked me what I wanted to be then told me what not to be. ... I was being told to accept the identity that others will give me.

Shane Koyczan

"When I was 5 years old, my mother always told me that happiness was the key to life.

When I went to school they asked me what I wanted to be when I grew up. I wrote down 'happy'.

They told me I didn't understand the assignment, and I told them they didn't understand life."

—John Lennon

3. Five O'Clock Whistle

If we learn to open our hearts, anyone, including the people who drive us crazy, can be our teacher. —Pema Chödrön

William Morgan had worked for more than thirty years. He paid his own way through college and now, in his late forties, felt the burden of working more frequently. William, a call center supervisor, shared an office with Simon, also a supervisor in the same division of Longview, Inc. They often worked together to evaluate employees, make reports to management, and compare notes about the day's events.

They had started on the same day at Longview, which now employed almost one thousand people. Longview was the region's second largest employer. They had the largest call center and a processing location as well. Both William and Simon started "under a headset" as they liked to say, taking calls and working up the ranks to client leader, team leader, tech leader, and finally to a supervisor role nearly three years ago.

Simon had a habit of uttering offhand and glib sounding statements, which William often found himself remembering and reflecting on. Last week at a lunch, Simon said, "What screws us up most in life is the picture in our heads of how things are supposed to be. Expectations are the devil!"

William had learned from Simon how words like *promise* and *request* held very specific meaning. When Amy said things like, "Those dishes in the sink aren't going to wash themselves," it was a request … sort of.

And how many times did William himself agree to do something with one of the boys, like have a catch or go to a movie, then end up not doing it? Was that a promise broken? Being specific and clear about requests and promises felt like zeroing in on a moving target—challenging, yes, but with precision it was a possible breakthrough connection in the making.

And as William shared more about his life over recent years, Simon's little sayings seemed to stick in William's head. He would sometimes drive all the way home without the radio on, not even noticing the silence as he remained in his thoughts.

Last week, William was telling Simon about his kids and how it felt like Tanner was more distant by the day. Amy was working more, and Steve was at college and uncertain about his major and not in any hurry to decide.

Simon responded by saying, "William, listen up. Live into your own promises, not up to other people's expectations."

William focused his mind. Did his expectations exceed his grasp? Expectations of a life well-lived for himself, and his family; a durable happiness; feeling he would truly achieve his purpose in the world. Accomplished? Satisfied? Others seemed to expect so much from William, and he felt he spent the vast majority of his time and energy meeting their expectations of him. What about his expectation of them, of himself?

When William left his childhood, he rarely looked back. He was not nostalgic about youth and at times consciously preferred being an adult. He pondered friends and colleagues who pined for high school and relished in reliving memories of youth. William found himself more often looking at the future and wanting to make promises to himself and his loved ones. It seemed to frustrate him more often lately when those expectations went unfulfilled.

Expectation

[ ]

Outcome [|] Disappointment

Expectation [|] Pleasant Surprise

Outcome [ ]

4. Dinnertime Conversation

I am who I am today because of the choices I made yesterday. —Eleanor Roosevelt

Steve Morgan was home again from college. His presence in the Morgan home had a different effect on different members of the family. His mother, Amy, was always pleased to see him, though the piles of laundry tempered that pleasure. Amy was always pleased to set another place or two for a family dinner.

Tanner would shrug and look away when seeing his older brother these days. Steve brought his girlfriend, Vanessa, who spent a few extra minutes catching up with Tanner. Vanessa was from a family of five kids, and as the oldest girl she had plenty of experience with younger siblings.

Tanner's mom, Amy, liked Vanessa. With no daughter and only boys in the house, Vanessa's more tender style occasionally reminded Amy what it might be like to have a daughter. Vanessa would often seem to gravitate to the room of the house where the person feeling most separate and isolated was and somehow had a way of drawing them back to the kitchen.

Vanessa was studying anthropology. Tanner just knew that she smelled good and usually appreciated her finding him in the garage, the back porch, or up in his room when everyone else was conversing and catching up with each other. That was where she found Tanner today, with the door only slightly open. She knocked and said hello.

"Hey, Vanessa."

"Whatcha doin'?"

"Nothing."

Vanessa leaned into the room without moving her feet. Tanner did not look up. "Hey, we learned this interesting thing about people and animals in a class I'm taking." She waited for any reaction and then continued, "Animals are instinctive; people make choices."

"Uh huh."

"Yeah," Vanessa continued despite no show of acknowledgement. "If you're aware enough to give yourself a choice, you can choose to look differently. You get to decide what has meaning and what doesn't and how much meaning and what it means."

"Wait, what?" Tanner was suddenly more conscious. "What about choices?"

"Life isn't about *finding* yourself, kid; it's about *creating* yourself. You create yourself through your choices." Vanessa stopped and leaned in a little more, her eyes meeting Tanner's for the first time that day.

"Wait a second," Tanner replied, fixing his eyes on Vanessa, "that actually makes sense."

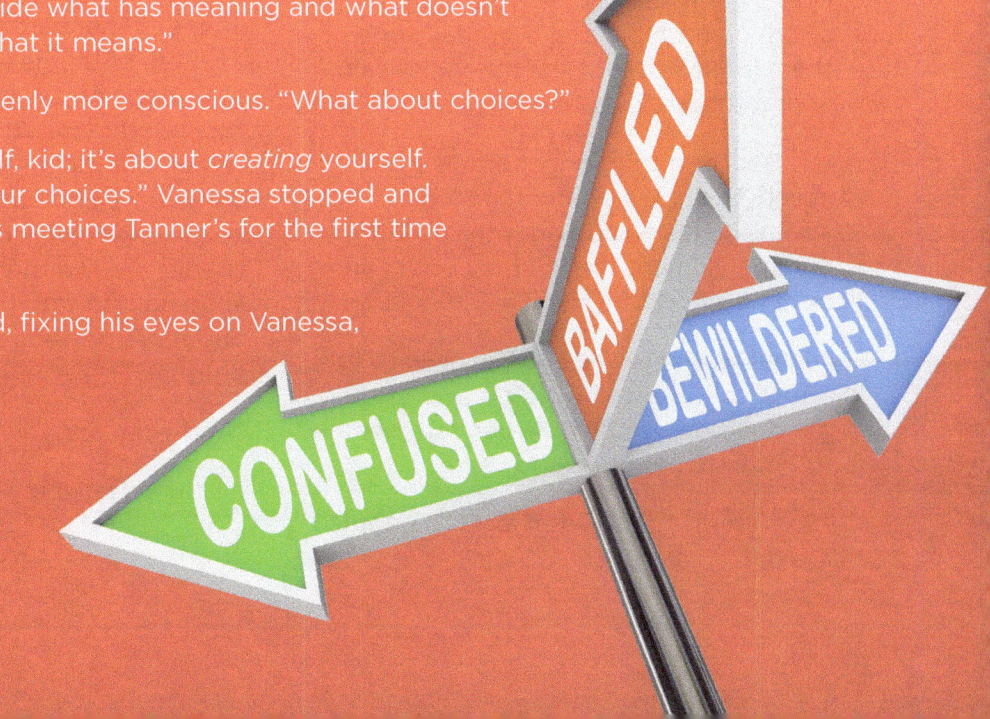

5. **Here and There**

A huge percentage of the stuff that I tend to be automatically certain of is, it turns out, totally wrong and deluded.
—David Foster Wallace

There were two young 🐠 swimming along, and they happened to meet an older 🐠 swimming the other way, who nodded at them and said, "Morning, boys. How's the water?" The two young 🐠 swam on for a bit, and eventually one of them looked over at the other and said, "What the heck is water?"

Ms. Goodwin told Tanner about a book called *This Is Water* and the story about the fish—and about the college commencement speech they both came from originally.

Tanner was in to see Ms. Goodwin to talk about colleges and working, and instead of the decisions getting clearer, they seemed to be getting more cloudy.

"So water is to fish what air is to people," figured Tanner.

"In part, in a certain kind of way. Do you think you relate more to the older 🐠, or the two younger 🐠🐠?" asked Melanie.

"Mmm, the older one, I guess," replied Tanner. "There are lots things like water, or air. Lots of things we don't notice until we start noticing them. I think I notice them more and more. And yet sometimes I can't remember if I ate breakfast or not, and some days I notice every person on the bus like we're in slow motion. And grades, grades are like this prophecy of our future seeping into today and noticing it more and more nowadays makes me feel, well, agitated."

"And what are you doing about it?"

"Well, I'm talking with you!"

PART TWO

6. The Glass

The highest reward for a person's toil is not what they get for it, but what they become by it. —John Ruskin

There once was a glass who didn't know if it was **half-full** or **half-empty**.

Who Am I: Individual Innovation 27

half-emp

Most of the glass's friends were half-empty and spent their time trying to fill themselves with fancy cars, expensive shoes and splendid watches. They tried to fill themselves with fancy friends and big houses.

The glass tried to fill itself up. But as much as it did... it always had half-way to go! So it said goodbye.

Then it met some friends who were half-full. They were busy working towards their goals, being responsible for themselves and to others and choosing their attitudes.

Half-full felt good for a while.

Then along came a glass that looked different than the others.

"Hello." said the glass.

"Hello."

"Are you half-full or half-empty?" asked the glass.

"I am more than half-full," said the other glass.

"What are you filled with?" asked the glass.

"Same as you. Maybe a little more of this or a little less of that."

"How did you get that way?"

The other glass carefully replied, "I keep my size steady. Then I take my fill slowly."

"Where did you come from?" asked the glass.

"Just over the other side of that hill."

"Can I go there?" wondered the glass.

"Perhaps. Well goodbye."

"Goodbye."

half-full

7. To Be or Not To Be

*If everyone is thinking alike,
then somebody isn't thinking.
—George S. Patton*

Imagine you are in a meeting with many important people. The boss comes in, takes a seat, and starts talking about "synergy in strategic markets" and "core competencies in vertical adjacencies."

To you, it sounds like nonsense. Maybe you're in the wrong meeting. Is anyone else confused?

Looking around the room, other people in attendance seem to be paying attention and nodding their head in agreement. How can this be?

They must know something you don't know.

Obviously, the best course of action at this point is to keep your mouth shut and say nothing. This should effectively hide what is likely your own lack of knowledge: A shrewd decision, perhaps, but it makes for a pretty dull life.

The famous soliloquy from Shakespeare's Hamlet, which begins "To be or not to be," has lessons for us all, and while we may not know what will become defining moments of our lives as they unfold in the instant, having a quantity of courage in ready supply will help.

to be or not to be?

Ms. Goodwin spent a few minutes sharing with Tanner how being "fearless" is not to be completely without fear, but rather to simply fear less. College and his future seemed to stoke the flames of fear for Tanner recently.

Tanner and Noah James talked over lunch about college visits and working over the summer, and without saying so, both knew there were decisions coming.

"Do you think things were easier in Shakespeare's time?" asked Noah James. "You know, didn't kids just become an apprentice in the family business, whatever it was?"

"Maybe," Tanner replied. "I suppose they had fewer choices to make."

"Yeah," added Noah James. "and Ms. Goodwin was saying about 'to do' and 'to be.' We spend more time on crossing things off our To-Do list than our To-Be list."

"To-Be list? I never heard of that," Tanner mentioned as he shifted to get up from the lunch table. "Sounds like something she would say," he continued. Maybe not a bad idea, he thought to himself, and he prepared for the afternoon of classes ahead.

8. Teaching and Learning

The true test of intelligence is not how much we know how to do, but how we behave when we don't know what to do.
—John Holt

William Morgan and Simon were attending a seminar titled "The Difference Between Learning by Instruction and Learning by Discovery."

The company they both worked for, Longview, was trying to improve itself. Occasionally Longview offered training classes for employees. Even more occasionally, Longview held required seminars for employees; this session was mandatory and held in the company cafeteria. There was a spiral packet placed on each chair, and William and Simon began reading.

To be informed is to **know** simply that something is the case. To be enlightened is to know, in addition, what it is all about: **why** it is the case, what its **connections** are with other facts, in what respects it is the same, in what respects it is different, and so forth. This is the difference between being able to remember something and being able to explain it."

Simon and William read silently as more colleagues entered and began to do the same.

If you remember what an author says, you have learned something from the reading. If what he says is true to you, you have learned something about the world. But whether it is a fact about the book or a fact about the world that you have learned, you have gained nothing but information if you have exercised only your memory.

You have not been enlightened.

Enlightenment is achieved only when, in addition to knowing what an author says, you have an opinion about **what** is meant and **why**—and more importantly you know what it means to **you**.

You can't be enlightened unless you know what it means for you; however you can be informed but not enlightened. Do you agree? Why or why not?

As much as William disliked missing the routine of his normal day, as well as usually being disappointed in the training programs he attended, he was quite engaged in the learning he experienced during the seminar.

As a supervisor, William was familiar with process thinking. He knew how following a defined process usually led to a predictable outcome. He thought the "Good" and "Bad" outcomes were enlightening (to use the phrase from the packet).

As he and Simon discussed their ideas and feedback on the course, William began to think how much of his day's lessons and messages fit into the whole of his life. He felt eager, for the first time in a long while, to get home and share something good from his day with Amy.

One of the final diagrams that the facilitators shared for the entire room to see and discuss was the following:

PART THREE

9. The Path

Biological evolution proceeds by a grand, inexorable process of trial and error—and without the errors the trials wouldn't accomplish anything.
—Daniel C. Dennett

Human beings are naturally diverse; we are not printed like coins all the same, but rather each and every one of us is both different and unique. Tanner sometimes felt like a sheep in a flock. At times he felt like a kind of creative burst was within his body, somehow searching to get out—like a balloon full of creative energy filling up and expanding.

Tanner had been encouraged by Vanessa to search the Internet for Sir Ken Robinson. "He is the king of creativity," she said.

Tanner found many videos, and the more he watched, the more drawn to the messages he became. He began to take notes of quotes from Sir Ken Robinson. Tanner thought they almost explained some of his own thinking better than he himself could.

"You were probably steered benignly away from things at school when you were a kid—things you liked—on the grounds that you would never get a job doing that: 'Don't do music, you're not going to be a musician. Don't do art, you won't be an artist.' Benign advice—now, profoundly mistaken."

—Sir Ken Robinson

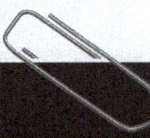

"If you're not prepared to be wrong, you'll never come up with anything original."

"All kids have tremendous talents—and we squander them pretty ruthlessly."

"Creativity now is as important in education as literacy, and we should treat it with the same status."

"I believe this passionately: that we don't grow into creativity, we grow out of it. Or rather, we get educated out if it."

"Many highly talented, brilliant, creative people think they're not—because the thing they were good at in school wasn't valued, or was actually stigmatized."

"There isn't an education system on the planet that teaches dance everyday to children the way we teach them mathematics. Why?"

"Typically [professors] live in their heads. . . . They look upon their body as a form of transport for their heads. It's a way of getting their head to meetings."

"We are educating people out of their creative capacities."

"You don't think of Shakespeare being a child, do you? Shakespeare being seven? He was seven at some point. He was in somebody's English class, wasn't he? How annoying would that be?"

"Very many people go through their whole lives having no real sense of what their talents may be, or if they have any to speak of."

"Human resources are like natural resources; they're often buried deep. You have to go looking for them, they're not just lying around on the surface."

"The dropout crisis is just the tip of an iceberg. What it doesn't count are all the kids who are in school but being disengaged from it, who don't enjoy it, who don't get any real benefit from it."

"Curiosity is the engine of achievement."

"The real role of leadership in education . . . is not and should not be command and control. The real role of leadership is climate control, creating a climate of possibility."

Very seldom is something created "right" the first time. Tanner's dad often told him that Edison spoke about finding 999 ways something didn't work before he found the one way it did.

Edison both failed and created magnificently. He held over one thousand patents and gave the world the light bulb. Tanner began to feel like the balloon building inside him was maybe a light bulb instead—growing brighter.

10. IF

> *In matters of style, flow like a river. In matters of principle, stand like a rock.*
> *—Thomas Jefferson*

What got you where you are won't get you where you are going. This latest aphorism from Simon was circling in William's mind as he drove home. Another day in the office had passed; another step down a path that seemed a bit hazy to William as it stretched forward. As his youngest boy, Tanner, was gearing toward leaving the house for college and Amy was back to work and really investing in her own career, William sometimes felt more like a passenger than the driver of his own life. Recent events had him poised to look at both what got him there and where he was going.

Tanner sat doing homework in the kitchen as William stepped into the house. William paused in the doorway of the dining room leading into the kitchen. Quietly, William walked over to his son, put his hand on Tanner's shoulder, and gave him a loving squeeze. Tanner sighed.

If you can keep your head when all about you
Are losing theirs and blaming it on you,
If you can trust yourself when all men doubt you,
But make allowance for their doubting too;
If you can wait and not be tired by waiting,
Or being lied about, don't deal in lies,
Or being hated, don't give way to hating,
And yet don't look too good, nor talk too wise:

If you can dream—and not make dreams your master;
If you can think—and not make thoughts your aim;
If you can meet with Triumph and Disaster
And treat those two impostors just the same;
If you can bear to hear the truth you've spoken
Twisted by knaves to make a trap for fools,
Or watch the things you gave your life to, broken,
And stoop and build 'em up with worn-out tools:

If you can make one heap of all your winnings
And risk it on one turn of pitch-and-toss,
And lose, and start again at your beginnings
And never breathe a word about your loss;
If you can force your heart and nerve and sinew
To serve your turn long after they are gone,
And so hold on when there is nothing in you
Except the Will which says to them: 'Hold on!'

If you can talk with crowds and keep your virtue,
Or walk with Kings—nor lose the common touch,
If neither foes nor loving friends can hurt you,
If all men count with you, but none too much;
If you can fill the unforgiving minute
With sixty seconds' worth of distance run,
Yours is the Earth and everything that's in it,
And—which is more—you'll be a Man, my son!

by Rudyard Kipling
("Brother Square-Toes"—Rewards and Fairies)

William could make out the name Kipling on Tanner's book. William knew of Kipling from his own school days; especially the classic poem "If." "If" was Kipling's four, eight-line stanzas of advice to his own son, written in 1909, inspiring its readers worldwide for over a century.

William could now see the poem on the page. He suddenly felt it was the perfect advice for a son born at the end of the last century, who would not know what triumphs and disasters lay ahead for him. It also put into words so much of what William himself was thinking and feeling. Tanner opened the text more widely, bending the book's spine to remove shadows from the page and creating both an invitation and request for his dad, one to which his dad made a silent and solemn promise for his son, himself, and their futures.

11. OPPOSITES

The world is not run by those who are right; it is run by those who can convince others they are right.
—Jamshid Gharajedaghi

"You might be surprised at what A.G. Lafley, Procter & Gamble's former CEO, can teach you about conversations," Melanie Goodwin stated as Tanner entered her office.

"In any conversation," she continued, knowing that Tanner was listening even as he settled in and opened his notebook, "business or personal, people tend to overuse one particular rhetorical tool at the expense of all the others. People's default style of communication tends to be advocacy—arguing in favor of their own perspective, statements about the truth of their own point of view. To create the kind of dialogue he wanted at P&G, people had to shift from that approach to a very different one."

A long pause. Tanner did not look up. Melanie was not at all uncomfortable with the quiet space. The air in the room seemed to settle pleasantly as the mood calmed.

Our own thinking
ADVOCACY

She continued, "The kind of dialogue he wanted to foster is called Assertive Inquiry, built on the work of organizational learning theorist Chris Argyris at Harvard Business School." Tanner continued taking notes without looking up. Melanie could tell he was listening and processing as she shifted in her chair, and Tanner kept focus on his writing. She opened a dry erase marker and turned in her chair to approach the white board behind her desk.

"This approach blends the explicit expression of your own thinking with a genuine exploration of the thinking of others. In other words, it means clearly articulating your own ideas and sharing your reasoning, while sincerely listening to the thoughts and reasoning of your peers." Melanie then wrote on her white board:

Thinking of others
INQUIRY

"To do this effectively, we need to embrace a certain stance about our own role in a discussion." Melanie stopped and waited for Tanner to look up. She turned from the whiteboard and slid a document across the desk to Tanner.

"This sounds like the reverse of what I usually do," admitted Tanner. "Trying to convince people is part of talking and explaining what you're thinking, isn't it?"

Melanie continued, "Well, perhaps it seems that way, but that may not be for the best. The plan at P&G was basically 'I have a view worth hearing, but I may be missing something.' It sounds simple, but this stance has a dramatic effect on group behavior if everyone in the room holds it."

"Hmm." Tanner picked his pen up and tapped it on his paper. "People try to explain their own thinking because they think they have a view worth hearing, so they advocate for their own perspective."

"Yes," added Melanie, "but because they remain open to the possibility that they may be missing something, two very important things happen. One, they advocate their view as a possibility, not as the single right answer. Two, they listen carefully and ask questions about alternative views. Why? Because, if they might be missing something, the best way to explore that possibility is to understand not what others see, but what they themselves do not see."

I think what Tanner thought was: "I think I get it: thinking I have the answer stops me from trying as hard, as does thinking that teachers, parents and adults have all the answers."

Melanie nodded her head. "Yes. Think about your friends or family who enter a conversation with the objective of convincing others they are right. They will advocate their position in the strongest possible terms, seeking to convince others and to win the argument. They will be less inclined to listen, or they will listen with the intent of finding flaws in the other people's arguments. This is a recipe for difficulty and discord."

Melanie pointed to the document on the desk as Tanner read it:

We wanted to open dialogue and increase understanding through a balance of advocacy and inquiry. This approach includes three key tools:

1. Advocating your own position and then inviting responses (e.g., "This is how I see the situation, and why; to what extent do you see it differently?");

2. Paraphrasing what you believe to be the other person's view and inquiring as to the validity of your understanding (e.g., "It sounds to me like your argument is this; to what extent does that capture your argument accurately?"); and

3. Explaining a gap in your understanding of the other person's views, and asking for more information (e.g., "It sounds like you think this acquisition is a bad idea. I'm not sure I understand how you got there. Could you tell me more?").

These kinds of phrases, which blend advocacy and inquiry, can have a powerful effect on the group dynamic. While it may feel more forceful to advocate, advocacy is actually a weaker move than balancing advocacy and inquiry. Inquiry leads the other person to genuinely reflect and hear your advocacy rather than ignoring it and making their own advocacy in response.

12. Finders Keepers

The first principle is that you must not fool yourself—and you are the easiest person to fool.
—Richard Feynman

"When Feynman faces a problem, he's unusually good at going back to being like a child; ignoring what everyone else thinks. He was so innovative; if something didn't work, he'd look at it another way." Simon was having a Feynman morning and shared his thoughts with William as usual.

Simon was a big fan of Richard Feynman, who was a theoretical physicist, Nobel laureate, and, perhaps most importantly, incurably curious. Simon had been noticing that William was dressing a little better, talking with more of his colleagues, and even coming up with more ideas. Simon was the recipient of many of those ideas.

Knowing William's youngest child was graduating from high school soon, Simon certainly understood what people sometimes called the empty nest syndrome. Amy was working more nowadays, Steve had a girlfriend and was making his way through college, and recently William had seemed listless at work.

Working life at Longview was moving forward day by day, month by month, and the balance between past, present, and future were matters of choice. Enthusiasm found in the early stages of employment, relationships, and even kids often gave way to satisfaction, complacency, and at times even smugness and resignation.

Simon often sang the praises of gratitude and the renewal of curiosity—finding a "good space" and keeping oneself in it. When he found someone in a good mood or a positive, grateful state of mind, Simon would tend to spend a few more minutes and linger longer, enjoying the space of positivity. Simon found himself lingering with William more than usual as William seemed to be finding and keeping himself in a place of purposeful, positive choice.

PART FOUR

13. Lost and Found

Just trust yourself, then you will know how to live.
—Johann Wolfgang von Goethe

"Why is it that I can listen to a song over and over again, but I get tired of reruns on TV?" Noah James wondered as he and Tanner rode the bus. "Isn't sight higher than hearing on the ranked scale of senses?"

"Songs seem to get into your soul, when you can find the right one. Not sure if TV can do that," Tanner offered.

Graduation was tomorrow, and this was one of the last bus rides the boys would take together. Tanner was still thinking about his latest discussion with Melanie. He was actually beginning to look forward to summertime and next year.

"Hey, don't forget we promised Melanie we'd watch Dead Poets Society today," reminded Noah James. "My house at 5:00 PM."

"Yep, see you then."

Both Tanner and Noah James had read poetry at the request of Melanie, and after a period of getting used to it were starting to more fully appreciate the sparse writing and deep meaning they found in her suggested reading, which included Walt Whitman.

She had clued them into the now-classic Robin Williams movie with a quote from one of the characters.

She shared it with the senior class in an e-mail earlier that week, which became something of a buzz as the final days approached.

To: Graduating Seniors

From: Melanie Goodwin

Subject: What Will Your Verse Be?

We don't read and write poetry because it's cute. We read and write poetry because we are members of the human race. And the human race is filled with passion. And medicine, law, business, engineering, these are noble pursuits and necessary to sustain life. But poetry, beauty, romance, love, these are what we stay alive for. To quote from Whitman: "O me! O life! … of the questions of these recurring; of the endless trains of the faithless—of cities filled with the foolish; what good amid these, O me, O life? Answer, That you are here—that life exists, and identity; that the powerful play goes on and you may contribute a verse." That the powerful play goes on and you may contribute a verse. What will your verse be?

—Tom Schulman,
from Dead Poets Society

"O Me! O Life!" from Whitman's Leaves of Grass (166)

O Me! O Life! . . . of the questions of these recurring;

Of the endless trains of the faithless——of cities fill'd with the foolish;

Of myself forever reproaching myself, (for who more foolish than I and who more faithless?)

Of eyes that vainly crave the light——of the objects mean—— of the struggle ever renew'd;

Of the poor results of all——of the plodding and sordid crowds I see around me;

Of the empty and useless years of the rest——with the rest me intertwined;

The question, O me! so sad, recurring——What good amid these, O me, O life?

Answer, That you are here——that life exists, and identity;

That the powerful play goes on, and you will contribute a verse.

The power and majesty of Whitman's verses gave Tanner goosebumps as he read and reread the e-mail. After they watched the film, Tanner went to his own journal and dusted off the verse he had been contemplating. It was a poem Tanner had started months ago and occasionally tinkered with, usually when the right mood of reflection and articulation descended onto him. Tanner stared at his poem, thinking about with whom he could share it. For Tanner, the words both beckoned toward the light of someone's reading and feedback, and simultaneously wanted to remain private and hidden in his own mind and heart.

Space for Gray

When we leave room for gray, we leave room for ourselves:
    the paradox of missing our past but being thrilled with the life we now lead,
    the contrast of striving for success through hard work,
    while knowing that rest, quiet and peaceful understanding can
        sometimes be the best path
    to our purpose.
The ambiguity of our future:
    knowing that we need to put ourselves in the best possible position,
    but also let go,
    that liminal space between our own defined selves
        and the culture of rules and expectations in which we live.
Life is not only in the good or bad,
    happy or sad,
    right or wrong,
    fast or slow,
    black or white.
It is in the space between, space where our spirit dwells,
    allowing us to be the contradiction that we are,
    allowing us to feel the spectrum of emotions life has to offer,
    not putting us into boxes of dichotomy.
For when we cope with fear of pain by creating a shell of indifference,
    we also numb our joys.
In the gray space between, there is room for pain and joy,
    love and hate,
    right and wrong.
There is room for others,
    there is room for courage,
    there is room for authenticity,
    there is room for us.

14. Next Conversation

Experience is not what happens to a man. It is what a man does with what happens to him.
—Aldous Huxley

Tanner found Melanie in her office. He had been a graduate for only a few hours and already it felt different to be in school—and to be in her office.

Still fresh from the hugs of family and friends, Tanner saw Melanie from a distance earlier but had not yet connected with her. "Hey," he said as he stepped into her office and sat in the familiar space.

"Congratulations, well done!" Melanie smiled.

Tanner felt her pride and warmth, though also a sudden, obvious realization that he was truly moving on.

"My e-mail address will stay the same," Melanie said as she sensed his trepidation. "It was great to see you and your family today; your mom and dad looked so happy."

"Yeah, we're going to dinner and I'm not dreading it," Tanner joked.

"Don't be a stranger, Mr. Tanner Morgan," Melanie said, "to me or yourself."

Tanner began to imagine the e-mail he might send to Melanie later that day, or later that summer, or later that year. "Thank you, for everything."

Afterword. Trail Forward

Tanner found that his experiences over the past few months were so formative, helpful, and consequential that he took his notebook and rewrote the key learnings. He also tried to record what related growth he felt and how it mattered to him.

Melanie went on to become the head of the guidance office at the high school. She and Tanner kept in touch via e-mail. Melanie encouraged Tanner to "pay it forward" when he expressed his thankfulness for all her help over the years. Tanner shared his writing with Melanie, and she encouraged him to share it further, suggesting that there were many teens, young adults, and even parents who might be interested in what and how he learned and what growth resulted.

Conversations are the most basic means of communications. While technology continues to advance to include paper, electronic, and other mediums, talking face to face always held particular value to Tanner. His record of his own transitions and the transitions of those around him was eventually organized into a text which could be shared. The specifics were slightly altered to maintain a level of privacy.

The text became fairly sought after in his immediate community, and then other local schools and even some workplaces began to reference some of the specifics. As the names were changed, there were only a few who believed they knew the true identities of the characters. Not that it mattered, as more and more communities found increasing value in reading, sharing, and talking about it.

Acknowledgments

This project involved a significant amount of effort, fun, and learning. Thanks to James Barnes for helping by being perhaps the most wonderful collaboration partner one could have expected. His energy, ideas, creativity, and demeanor all became treasures to me. I am fortunate for his enduring friendship.

Thanks also to family and friends whose support and feedback were always welcome, particularly Christie Barnes, who seemed always eager to help. Particular appreciation to Sharon for her continuing and valued engagement and love. Shout-outs to Randi and Troy.

Special recognition for Kerra Henkin and Brad Henkin: You are both blessings, and I hope our paths will only grow closer and more devoted in learning and love.

—DGH

My gratitude starts to David—the vast majority of the industry in this book has been his. David has been a friend, colleague, student, coachee, co-teacher, and now co-author, and in all of these roles, my experience has been one of learning from and with him. David is always curious, ever analytical, a seeker of meaning, searching for ways to help others and open to having fun. This latest collaboration has been a gift. Thank you, David.

My second thank you is to the reader, whatever your purpose. My hope is that this fable sparks some ideas and action to help you accomplish your purpose in the world. Please go to JBInnovation.com and share in a blog post ideas sparked by this book and how you have put them to use. Thanks to my U.K family and special thanks to my U.S. family, Buff, Mike, Julie, Christie, Katie, Andy, Henry, and Hemsley for their unerring support and inspiration. A shout out to Christie, whose encouragement and ideas as my TA for innovation class (all the way from China) have been so valuable. Christie also penned the words to Tanner's poem.

Finally, thanks to my students at Villanova for the serious fun. You have taught me more than you know!

—JRB

www.ingramcontent.com/pod-product-compliance
Lightning Source LLC
Chambersburg PA
CBHW080520300426
44112CB00018B/2811